Series 7 Exam Prep

2023-2024

The Ultimate Study Guide for Acing the Serie 7 Exam on Your First Try | Secrets and Expertly Crafted Strategies with 6 Practice Test Simulations and Video Lessons

Niles Norris

Table of Contents

Introduction

In the vast world of finance, the Series 7 Exam stands as a formidable barrier between aspiring professionals and their dreams of success. Its complex web of rules, regulations, and mind-boggling calculations can make even the most seasoned individuals feel like they're drowning in a sea of financial jargon. But fear not, dear reader, for within the pages of this book lies the key to unlocking your true potential and conquering the Series 7 Exam once and for all.

Picture this: you're sitting in a sterile, windowless room, nervously clutching a pencil as you prepare to embark on the exam that could determine the course of your career. The weight of responsibility bears down on your shoulders, and the butterflies in your stomach are threatening to break free. You've spent countless hours studying, yet doubt creeps in. Will you be able to recall all the intricate details and apply them correctly under the immense pressure?

If this scenario strikes a chord with you, then you're not alone. The Series 7 Exam is notorious for its rigorous nature, leaving many candidates overwhelmed, confused, and downright terrified. But fear not, for I have personally experienced the struggles and triumphs of this exam, and I am here to guide you through every step of the way.

This book is not just a dry collection of facts and formulas. No, it is a lifeline for those drowning in a sea of financial complexity. It understands your pain, your struggles, and your burning desire to succeed. With this book in your hands, you will gain the knowledge, confidence, and strategy necessary to tackle the Series 7 Exam with unwavering determination.

So, what can you expect from this comprehensive guide? Prepare to dive deep into the intricate world of securities and financial regulations. You will learn how to navigate the maze of complex concepts, from options and margin accounts to municipal bonds and investment strategies. This book will be your compass, guiding you through the treacherous terrain of the Series 7 Exam syllabus.

Now, you may be wondering, "Why should I trust this author to lead me on this journey?" Fair question. Allow me to introduce myself. I am [Author's Name], a seasoned financial professional with years of experience in the industry. I have not only triumphed over the Series 7 Exam myself but have also helped countless others achieve their goals. My expertise in the subject matter, combined with my passion for teaching and guiding aspiring professionals like yourself, makes me the ideal mentor on your path to success.

As you turn the pages of this book, you will feel an unmistakable connection. The conversational tone, the relatable examples, and the carefully crafted explanations will make you think, "This is the right book for me." Gone are the days of confusion and uncertainty. With each chapter, you will gain the knowledge and confidence necessary to overcome any challenge the Series 7 Exam throws your way.

So, dear reader, it is time to embark on this transformative journey. Get ready to conquer your fears, harness your potential, and emerge as a victorious conqueror of the Series 7 Exam. The path to success awaits you, and this book will be your trusted guide every step of the way. Let us begin.

Chapter 1: Understanding The Serie 7 Exam: Objectives, Structure, And Scoring

What is the Series 7 Exam?

The General Securities Representative Examination, often known as the Series 7 Exam, is administered in the US by the Financial Industry Regulatory Authority (FINRA). Its goal is to assess a general securities representative's ability to perform their work tasks. Stockbrokers or registered representatives are other names for general securities representatives.

The Series 7 Exam is one of the most comprehensive and challenging exams accessible for people seeking to become registered representatives. It addresses a broad variety of issues related to the securities industry. Each of the two sections of the exam contains 125 multiple-choice questions. The exam is divided into two parts: the first portion covers investment risk, taxation, equities and debt instruments, packaged securities, options, and retirement plans, while the second part looks at regulatory requirements, customer accounts, and prohibited activities.

To pass the Series 7 Exam, a candidate must receive a score of at least 72%. The exam is regularly taken by those who want to work as registered representatives at brokerage firms and sell a variety of securities products to clients. To register as a general securities representative in the US, you must pass the Series 7 Exam.

Understanding the Series 7 Examinations

1. The main purpose of the Series 7 exam is to make sure that candidates for registration as general securities representatives have a basic comprehension of the laws, rules, and ideas that govern the securities business. Their understanding of trading, customer accounts, investment products, and professional conduct are all tested.

2. There are 125 multiple-choice questions in the Series 7 exam, and applicants have 225 minutes (3 hours and 45 minutes) to do it. The exam includes information on a wide range of subjects, including as equities, debt securities, options, investment firms, retirement plans, taxation, and regulation.

3. Candidate must receive a passing score of 72 percent or above on the Series 7 exam in order to pass. Depending on how many questions were correctly answered, a score is assigned. There is no penalty for providing a wrong answer because each question is given the same weight.

4. Study Aids: In order to prepare for the Series 7 exam, candidates frequently use study aids offered by training companies. Online resources, practice tests, and textbooks are frequently included in these products. To boost your chances of success, it is advised that you set aside enough time to study and review the material.

5. Individuals must be connected to a FINRA member firm in order to be eligible to take the Series 7 exam. Typically, in order to register for the exam, candidates need to be sponsored by the company where they are employed. The Securities Industry Essentials (SIE) test is one possible prerequisite that they could also need to pass.

6. Continuing Education: To keep your registration active after passing the Series 7 exam, you must take part in continuous continuing education (CE) programs. Registered representatives can stay current on industry developments, rules, and best practices by participating in CE programs.

7. Possibilities for Careers Possibilities for employment in the securities business are increased by passing the Series 7 exam. Stockbrokers, financial consultants, investment consultants, and other positions requiring the sale and trading of securities are all positions that registered representatives are qualified to fill.

Series 7 Exam Requirements

Sponsorship: To be eligible for the Series 7 exam, you must be sponsored by a FINRA member firm. This means you need to be employed by a brokerage firm or a financial institution that is registered with FINRA.

Age: There is no minimum age requirement set by FINRA to take the Series 7 exam. However, individual firms may have their own minimum age requirements, typically ranging from 18 to 21 years old.

Regulatory Exams: Before taking the Series 7 exam, you must pass the Securities Industry Essentials (SIE) exam, which covers basic securities industry knowledge. The SIE exam is a prerequisite for all individuals seeking to become registered representatives.

Education: There are no specific educational requirements to take the Series 7 exam. However, most firms require a high school diploma or equivalent.

U.S. Residency or Citizenship: You do not have to be a U.S. citizen or a permanent resident to take the Series 7 exam. However, you must have a valid U.S. Social Security number.

Criminal Background Check: You may be subject to a background check as part of the registration process. Certain criminal convictions may disqualify you from taking the exam or obtaining registration.

Essential Information on the Series 7 Examination

A minimum score of 72 percent is required to pass and acquire a Series 7 license (equal to a C- grade). In order to guarantee that you are adequately prepared for the real exam while working toward your license, you should generally aim for a practice exam score of at least 80 to 85 percent.

What is the Exam's Difficulty Level: Even though Series 7 may appear frightening if you have no work experience, it is a relatively difficult test. No of their level of experience, anyone can ace the exam with enough preparation time. On average, 65 percent of applicants succeed on the Series 7 exam.

You are free to take the test as many times as you like. There are rules about the amount of time between trials, though. The standard rule is that you must wait at least 30 days between your initial and subsequent test attempts. You must wait at least six months or 180 days before trying again after a third unsuccessful attempt.

Weekdays you should take your exams: As long as you schedule a testing time in advance, you are permitted to take the Series 7 on any weekday. Prior to scheduling an appointment with one of the recognized testing centers, such as Pearson VUE or Prometric, Form U-4 must be submitted to open a window with FINRA. You must arrive 30 minutes prior to the exam's scheduled start time so that you have enough time to prepare. Bring a government-issued photo ID with you to check in, such as a passport or driver's license, and be prepared to have your fingerprints taken. You must store your personal items in the available lockers because they are not permitted in the test room. You will be given a calculator, earplugs, pencil, scratch paper, markers, and dry-erase sheets at the exam site.

Test Results: After submitting your test answers, you will receive your test results right away. FINRA, the central registration depository of FINRA, will finally get in touch with the testing facility and deliver this information to your business using Web CRD.

The Tested Subjects are Examined.

You will be required to handle client accounts, know the laws governing the securities industry, and perform specific mathematical calculations as part of the Series 7 practical test.

Chapter 2: Study Strategies For Excelling In The Exam

When it comes to excelling in exams, having effective study strategies can make a significant difference in your performance. Here are some strategies that can help you prepare effectively:

- Plan your study time: Make a calendar that allots precise time intervals for each subject or topic so you may schedule your study time in advance. You can stay organized and make sure you cover all the relevant stuff if you do this.

- Dissect the content: Break up your reading content into digestible sections. By dividing it down, you may concentrate on one subject at a time, which makes it simpler to comprehend and recall the data.

- Use active learning strategies: Active learning strategies should be used in place of passive reading or listening to the material. This can involve writing a personal summary of the material, imparting it to others, making flashcards, or resolving practice problems.

- Practice with previous tests or practice papers: Utilize former tests or sample papers to familiarize yourself with the format and types of questions that may be asked on the test. This will enable you to get used to the exam format and pinpoint your areas for development.

- Ask for clarification: Don't be afraid to ask your teachers, classmates, or internet resources for help if you run into concepts or subjects that you don't quite grasp. Your capacity to perform well on the exam will improve after properly understanding the topic.

- Take frequent rests: Even though studying for long periods of time may feel beneficial, frequent breaks are necessary to prevent burnout and retain attention. Taking little pauses might help you mentally refresh and increase productivity.

- Use mnemonic tools to help you remember complex material. Mnemonics are memory strategies. Make rhymes, illustrations, or acronyms to go along with important terms, formulas, or ideas.

- Remain arranged: Organize your notes, resources, and study materials. When you need to review or refer back to certain information, you will save time and experience less stress if you have this system in place. To increase your speed and accuracy, practice answering questions in a limited amount of time. This will enable you to finish the exam within the allotted time.

- Take care of yourself: A healthy lifestyle is crucial for achieving your best results. Get enough rest, eat healthful meals, and work out frequently. Your capacity to focus and recall knowledge will improve if you take care of your physical and mental health.

Many candidates getting ready to take the Series 7 exam haven't had to prepare for a test in a long time. Even the most experienced students may struggle with Series 7's demanding knowledge requirements.

Many candidates study for additional exams or become familiar with the policies of their firm in order to land a job in addition to preparing for their Series 7 exam. Time management is essential. Check out some of the different approaches this chapter offers, even if you think you know how to approach your study. You might come upon a test-taking strategy that works better.

What Kind of Student Are You?

You should take your preferred learning method into account while creating a study plan. Studying involves more than just reading and underlining texts. The optimum use of your time can be achieved by being aware of the many methods for information retention.

Think about the techniques you have previously employed to learn new things. Do you like listening to lectures? You are therefore an auditory learner. Do you prefer to read? Visual learning must be your preferred method of learning. Or is the best way to learn by doing something like creating a client profile? Touch is the best way to learn.

Adapt your study strategies to your preferred learning style to get the most out of your study time.

Studying Methods

For many people, combining a few of these techniques is the best approach to learning new material. Combining various study techniques can enable you to plan your study time more effectively and avoid burnout. Look at several teaching methods to see which one is best for you.

Try some of these methods for learning that use the auditory, visual, and tactile senses:

Auditory Learning Techniques:

- Recite difficult-to-remember content; repetition can help you remember the formulas you'll need to calculate exam responses.

- recite something while recording it. You can listen to it while driving home or while working out by playing it back on an MP3 device.

- To help you remember rules or formulas, use rhymes or acronyms.

Visual Learning Techniques:

- Make notes, diagrams, or checklists to visually summarize the information.

- As you read, mark important passages with highlighters.

Tactile/Kinesthetic Learning Techniques:

- Make a fictitious client profile and apply the knowledge gained during a fictitious counseling session. If you'd like, you can model this customer profile after a real-life or imagined client.

- Utilize the formulas in this book to translate theoretical ideas into real-world situations. Use the sample questions and examples if you're having trouble understanding the text because they make more sense to tactile learners.

- While studying, get up and move.

Study Groups

The number of registered representatives at your company may go beyond simply you. Your other Series 7 applicants will be a tremendous source of support if this is the situation. You could even wish to work together to form a study group.

If you learn best by using your hands, study groups may be helpful. Help from other applicants may be helpful if you're having trouble understanding a particular piece of information. Here are some suggestions for making the most of your study time together if you decide to form a group. You may also use them to manage your own study time.

- Maintain a timetable with a set start and end time.

- To save time and stay in touch with the entire study group at once, use group texting.

- Avoid places that can be distracting, such as restaurants or other public areas. If your library or local coffee shop has a meeting area available, see if you can reserve it.

- Set specific objectives for the topics you want to address at each meeting. Think about making a study schedule (more on how to create one later in this chapter).

- You can rotate between group members as the leader for each meeting to keep everyone on track.

Each member of the study group must be intensely focused on their objective for the group to be successful. Remind any group members who are particularly disruptive of your shared objective—passing the test—if necessary. However, politely excuse yourself from the study session and carry on alone if you discover that it is not the best use of your time. Keep in mind that passing the exam, not having fun, is your main priority.

A word of caution: Group study is not recommended when preparing for the Series 7 test. Since you will be taking the test alone and the subject is difficult and theoretical, it is advisable to study alone to save time. Study groups run the risk of turning into social meetings, taking up time that would be better spent studying alone.

Before starting or joining a study group to get ready for your Series 7 exam, give it some thought.

Breaking It Down

As stated in the introduction, each of the five critical functions is weighed differently on the test by the number of questions — and you can use this to your advantage.

If you are in a time crunch, or have to decide which portions to review, study those items that carry the most weight. Look at the listings of the five critical functions in this book's introduction to see how the exam is weighted.

Other ways to break the study material into manageable chunks include:

- Using the checklists and bold text blocks in this book to test your knowledge. Once you have determined you know something, move on. There is no need to review something you already know; once is enough.

- Creating index cards on different subjects. You can use this book's bold words for condensed information. With these index cards, you have small chunks of studying material ready for those 15 minutes in line at the DMV, those 10 minutes in the car waiting for your kids to get out of school, etc. This technique is great for applicants lacking big blocks of study time. Make sure you carry these index cards with you wherever you go.

- Ensuring you know how to make calculations. You can miss a question or two on theoretical knowledge and still pass, but you will have to be able to calculate numbers like how much a stock is in-the-money or the value of a stock after a split. If you are in a time crunch, focus on the formulas and make sure you know how to apply them.

What to Expect on Testing Day

Testing day does not have to be as stressful as you may think. The best way to study is to practice taking the exam using the mock exam in this book and to know what to expect on testing day.

Get a good night's rest, eat a healthy breakfast, and dress for comfort on testing day.

First, you need to make sure you bring everything you need to the testing center:

- A sack lunch and any snacks to eat during your break (try to keep these healthy to fuel your body)
- Government-issued ID; make sure your name matches the name you used to register for the exam
- Study material, like notes or index cards you made, so you can brush up on material while you wait
- A watch

You will not be allowed to bring in bags, purses, study materials, or electronic devices (like cell phones) into the test room. The exam center will give you a calculator, six pieces of letter-sized paper (or a whiteboard), and a pencil for use in each session.

The testing center employee will guide you to a cubicle where you will begin your test. Once the clock starts, you need to make sure you use your time wisely.

Owning Your Time

Your Series 7 exam divides the 260 questions between two three-hour blocks. There is a mandatory 30 to 60 minute break between the two blocks. Once you sign out after the first session, you cannot go back and change any answers.

You are allowed to take breaks during your exam, but your exam time is not paused for this. Avoid drinking a lot of water or other liquids so you are not wasting valuable time taking bathroom breaks.

Once you sit down to answer questions, it is important to break your allotted three hours into smaller segments. These segments will help you make sure you are on track.

To make sure you are on track on your test, try to complete at least 44 questions per hour, or one minute and 20 seconds on each question.

Series 7 exams are designed to give you ample time to finish each test portion. As long as you have studied and know the material, there is no reason for you not to finish your exam on time — provided you do not panic or make other mistakes that slow you down.

To move from question to question at a steady pace, there are a few test-taking tricks you can use:

Read carefully. It is easy to miss a word (for example, "except"), and get the question wrong.

Take your time to understand what is being asked.

1. Do not get stuck on one question. If you are unsure of the answer, mark the question for review and move on.
2. Use the process of elimination if you are unsure of the answer. Questions are usually designed to have two completely wrong answers and two that are close to correct.
3. Every question is scored, so even if you have no idea what the answer is, guess. Unanswered questions are counted as a wrong answer.
4. When in doubt, trust your gut. Your first choice is often the right one — do not make the mistake of over-thinking a question and changing a right answer to a wrong one.

The minute you start the test, use one sheet of scrap paper to write down any formulas you remember. This will relax your mind and allow you to focus on the questions.

Nerves can do a number on your mind, and it can be difficult to clear your mind enough to answer questions correctly. Releasing the stress of retaining information will allow you to focus on your test.

Chapter 3: Time Management And Motivation During Preparation

Time Management

As you will soon find as a registered representative, time management is a crucial component to any task. Whether you are studying or marketing to new customers, you will find managing your time wisely will benefit you in the long run.

1. Familiarize yourself with the exam structure: Understand the format of the exam, including the number of questions, types of questions, and the allocated time. This will help you plan your time accordingly.

2. Read the instructions carefully: Before you begin answering any questions, carefully read the instructions for each section. Understand the requirements and how much time you should allocate to each section.

3. Plan your time: Allocate a specific amount of time for each question or section based on its marks or complexity. This will help you stay on track and ensure you don't spend too much time on one question at the expense of others.

4. Start with easier questions: Begin by answering the questions you find easier or are more confident about. This will help you gain momentum and save time for the more challenging questions later on.

5. Avoid spending excessive time on a single question: If you encounter a difficult question, don't dwell on it for too long. Move on to the next question and come back to it later if time permits. Remember, you can always make educated guesses and come back to review your answers during the remaining time.

6. Stay focused and avoid distractions: Minimize distractions such as your phone, social media, or unnecessary conversations during the exam. Stay focused on the task at hand to make the most of your time.

7. Monitor your progress: Keep an eye on the clock or your allocated time for each section. If you're falling behind, adjust your pace accordingly. It's better to complete all the questions, even if you need to rush a bit, rather than leaving some questions unanswered.

8. Review your answers: If you finish the exam early, use the remaining time to review your answers. Check for any errors or omissions and make necessary revisions if needed. This step is crucial to improve your overall accuracy.

9. Practice time management during preparation: Develop good time management skills during your exam preparation as well. By practicing timed mock tests or solving previous years' question papers within the specified time limits, you can improve your speed and efficiency.

How to Create a Studying Schedule

Before you dig into the studying material, make sure you have a plan of attack. Here is a simple way to create a schedule:

- Take your planner or a printed calendar (some computer software carry a calendar-printing function) and look at how many days you have from today until testing day.

- Using the breakdown you made of this book's chapters, divide the portions evenly among your calendar days, leaving the last two or three days for your practice test and review.

- Estimate how much time studying each portion will take, adding time for breaks if necessary.

- Decide when you will be studying. Schedule study time just like you would schedule an important meeting.

Your studying schedule is your tool to stay on track. If you follow your schedule, you will be ready on testing day.

Once you begin studying, keep track of how much time you studied and how much progress you made. Do you need more or less time than you thought? Adjust your schedule accordingly.

On the opposite page is an example of what your studying schedule might look like. Note how there is room to chart progress, to give a clear view of what was accomplished, and what still needs to be done.

Note how this schedule did not plan any study time for Sunday. Although it is important to take studying seriously, you should also schedule breaks and the occasional day off.

Allow time in your schedule for breaks and for days off if possible. Breaks give you a chance to recharge and be more productive when you sit down to study again.

Quick Studying Tips

Your new studying schedule may overwhelm you when you see all the hard work you have ahead. Here are some quick tips to make studying a little easier:

- If you must forgo certain commitments, family or personal, explain to those involved that you are studying for an important exam. If you have children, reassure them that this imposition is only temporary. You can show them on a calendar when your test day is scheduled. Make sure you allow yourself time to enjoy some of your normal leisurely activities, to keep a balance with your rigorous studies.

- Find a quiet spot to study away from TV, Internet, or other distractions. If you live in a noisy house, consider playing soft music to drown out distracting sounds. And if you have trouble with procrastinating on your devices, try an app or browser extension that temporarily blocks internet access.

- Use the checklists and study plan in this book to chart your progress. Crossing off a subject as you finish it can be a very satisfying way to chart your progress.

- Eat well and get plenty of sleep. Your mind needs nourishment and rest to function at its best.

- If you are motivated by reward, consider promising yourself something nice when you pass the test, like a day out with the family or dinner at your favorite restaurant.

Motivation During Preparation

Preparing for the Series 7 exam can be a demanding and challenging task. It requires a significant amount of time, effort, and dedication to succeed. To stay motivated throughout the preparation process, consider the following factors:

1. Career advancement: Passing the Series 7 exam is often a requirement for many financial professionals, particularly those working in securities trading or brokerage firms. Earning this certification can open up new opportunities for career growth, higher salaries, and job promotions.

2. Expanded knowledge and expertise: The Series 7 exam covers a wide range of topics related to securities and investments. As you study for the exam, you'll gain a deeper understanding of financial markets, regulations, investment products, and client interactions. This knowledge will not only benefit you during the exam but also enhance your professional competence in the long run.

3. Personal growth and achievement: Successfully passing the Series 7 exam is a significant accomplishment. It demonstrates your dedication, hard work, and ability to acquire complex knowledge in the financial industry. The sense of personal achievement and the boost to your self-confidence can serve as powerful motivators during your exam preparation.

4. Long-term financial rewards: A strong performance on the Series 7 exam can lead to increased earning potential and financial rewards. The certification enables you to work with a broader range of clients and offers a wider array of investment products. With increased expertise and a professional designation, you may attract more clients and generate higher commissions or fees.

5. Support from peers and mentors: Surrounding yourself with like-minded individuals who are also preparing for the Series 7 exam can be highly motivating. Join study groups, online forums, or seek out mentorship from experienced professionals who have already passed the exam. Sharing your

challenges, discussing strategies, and receiving encouragement from others can help you stay motivated and accountable.

6. Visualize success: Imagine yourself successfully passing the Series 7 exam and reaping the rewards that come with it. Visualize the sense of accomplishment, the opportunities that will arise, and the personal and professional growth that will accompany your success. This mental imagery can provide a powerful motivational boost when you encounter difficulties or feel overwhelmed.

7. Break it down: Preparing for the Series 7 exam can be overwhelming due to the volume of material to cover. Break down your study plan into smaller, manageable tasks and set specific goals for each study session. Celebrate your progress along the way and take pride in completing each step towards your ultimate goal of passing the exam.

Remember to maintain a healthy work-life balance throughout your preparation. Take breaks, exercise, and engage in activities that recharge your energy and help you stay focused. By staying motivated, maintaining discipline, and following a structured study plan, you can increase your chances of success in the Series 7 exam.

Chapter 4: Essential Financial Regulations For The Series 7 Exam

A minimum score of 72 percent is required to pass and acquire a Series 7 license (equal to a C- grade). In order to guarantee that you are adequately prepared for the real exam while working toward your license, you should generally aim for a practice exam score of at least 80 to 85 percent.

What is the Exam's Difficulty Level: Even though Series 7 may appear frightening if you have no work experience, it is a relatively difficult test. No of their level of experience, anyone can ace the exam with enough preparation time. On average, 65 percent of applicants succeed on the Series 7 exam.

You are free to take the test as many times as you like. There are rules about the amount of time between trials, though. The standard rule is that you must wait at least 30 days between your initial and subsequent test attempts. You must wait at least six months or 180 days before trying again after a third unsuccessful attempt.

Weekdays you should take your exams: As long as you schedule a testing time in advance, you are permitted to take the Series 7 on any weekday. Prior to scheduling an appointment with one of the recognized testing centers, such as Pearson VUE or Prometric, Form U-4 must be submitted to open a window with FINRA. You must arrive 30 minutes prior to the exam's scheduled start time so that you have enough time to prepare. Bring a government-issued photo ID with you to check in, such as a passport or driver's license, and be prepared to have your fingerprints taken. You must store your personal items in the available lockers because they are not permitted in the test room. You will be given a calculator, earplugs, pencil, scratch paper, markers, and dry-erase sheets at the exam site.

Test Results: After submitting your test answers, you will receive your test results right away. FINRA, the central registration depository of FINRA, will finally get in touch with the testing facility and deliver this information to your business using Web CRD.

Financial Industry Regulatory Authority regulations (FINRA) The Series 7 test will cover all of the FINRA-established guidelines for appropriateness, public communications, anti-money laundering (AML), supervision, and ethical standards.

The Blue-Sky Laws and the Uniform Securities Act of the United States The majority of states have adopted the USA model law for state-level securities regulation. A possible component of the Series 7 test involves US law, such as registration requirements, exemptions, antifraud laws, and remedies. You should also be familiar with the Blue-Sky Laws, which are state-specific securities regulations.

The Securities Investor Protection Act (SIPA) created the Securities Investor Protection Corporation to safeguard clients in the event that broker-dealers fail (SIPC). For the recovery of funds and securities held by clients in closed brokerage firms, it offers restricted coverage.

Dodd-Frank In reaction to the financial crisis of 2008, Congress passed the Consumer Protection and Wall Street Reform Act. It makes an effort to improve consumer protection, transparency, and financial regulation. The Volcker Rule, over-the-counter derivatives regulation, and the creation of the Consumer Financial Protection Bureau are just a few examples of the subjects that the Series 7 examination may touch on (CFPB).

Programs to identify customers and practice "Know Your Customer" Financial institutions are required by these regulations to confirm the legitimacy of their clients and determine whether they are suitable for investing. You need to be familiar with the guidelines and practices for KYC and CIP.

Regulatory controls to stop money laundering (AML) Money laundering and terrorism financing through the use of financial systems are prohibited under anti-money laundering laws (AML). Due diligence on customers, reporting suspicious conduct, and creating AML compliance procedures may all be included in the Series 7 exam.

In order to pass the Series 7 exam, you need review these and other significant financial regulations. The best course of action is to consistently consult the most recent study guides provided by FINRA, as the exam's curriculum and substance are susceptible to change over time. .

Chapter 5: Ethics And Professional Responsibilities In The Financial Industry

In order to ensure the dependability, accountability, and trustworthiness of financial institutions and staff, ethics and professional obligations are vital. Upholding moral standards is essential for keeping the public's faith in the sector and encouraging long-term sustainable growth. Some fundamental components of moral conduct and professional responsibility in the financial business include the following:

Financial advisors have a fiduciary duty to act in their clients' best interests and to prioritize their needs over their own. You must provide unbiased advice, avoid conflicts of interest, and be honest about any current or potential conflicts in order to meet this commitment.

Honesty & Integrity: Financial professionals should act with the utmost honesty and integrity while interacting with customers, employees, and other stakeholders. They must act honestly at all times, avoid making false comments, and communicate in a clear and accurate manner.

Financial professionals are obligated to follow strict privacy standards and protect customer information's confidentiality. They must handle client data with care and keep it safe from unauthorized access or disclosure.

Financial professionals must abide by laws, rules, and industry norms in order to practice legally. This calls for observing regulations governing trading, investing, and reporting practices as well as anti-money laundering (AML) and know your customer (KYC) standards.

Professional Competence: Financial professionals should always advance their knowledge and abilities to ensure that they provide their clients with competent advice and services. They should stay up to date on industry trends, governmental developments, and best practices through ongoing education and professional development.

Avoiding Insider Trading: It is against the law for financial experts to trade stocks based on significant non-public information. They must adhere to insider trading laws and properly segregate their access to sensitive information from their individual trading activities.

Management of Conflicts of Interest: Financial professionals should proactively identify and manage conflicts of interest to ensure that they do not compromise the best interests of customers. This means exposing potential conflicts of interest, putting in place adequate safeguards, and making decisions that prioritize the welfare of the clients.

Financial professionals have a responsibility to preserve social justice, safeguard the environment, and advance a flourishing society. They should promote sustainable financial practices and consider how their decisions may impact different stakeholders.

Professionalism and Courtesy: Financial professionals should conduct themselves in a professional manner while being considerate of others, including their clients, coworkers, and clients. They ought to abstain from discriminatory conduct, support inclusion and diversity, and foster a friendly workplace.

Whistleblower protection: People in the financial sector should have their rights preserved and supported if they disclose unethical behavior or wrongdoing. Fostering an open culture and safeguarding whistleblowers are essential for identifying and correcting any ethical infractions.

It is essential for financial professionals and institutions to establish robust ethical frameworks, provide comprehensive training on ethical standards, and enforce accountability for unethical behavior. Regulating bodies and industry associations have a key role in establishing and sustaining ethical standards within the financial sector. .

Chapter 6: Securities Analysis: Fundamentals And Evaluation Strategies

Fundamental Analysis:

To study fundamentals, one must consider the underlying factors that have an impact on an investment's value. This approach takes the company's financial health and potential for future growth into account when determining whether a stock is undervalued or overvalued. Some essential components of fundamental analysis include the following:

monetary statements The balance sheet, income statement, and cash flow statement are the three financial statements that can be used to evaluate a business's stability, profitability, and ability to generate cash flow.

Ratios and Metrics To gain insights into a company's performance and market worth, financial ratios and measures like the price-to-earnings (P/E), price-to-sales (P/S), return on equity (ROE), and debt-to-equity ratio can be computed and assessed.

By assessing the competitive environment, industry trends, and market circumstances, it is easier to analyze a company's position within its industry and its growth potential.

Management and Governance: A company's ability to implement its business strategy can be evaluated by closely examining the skills and experience of its management team, as well as its corporate governance procedures and strategic objectives.

Macroeconomic Factors: It is feasible to forecast how a company's operations will be impacted by the state of the market and more general economic variables like interest rates, inflation, and geopolitical circumstances.

Evaluation Strategies:

Examining the underlying factors that influence a security's value is a component of fundamental analysis. This method assesses a company's financial health and potential for future growth to determine whether its stock is undervalued or overvalued. The following is a list of some crucial components of fundamental analysis:

Financial Statements: Examining a company's financial accounts, which include the balance sheet, income statement, and cash flow statement, can provide information about its liquidity, profitability, and cash flow generation.

Measurements and Ratios By calculating and analyzing various financial ratios and indicators, including as the price-to-earnings (P/E), price-to-sales (P/S), return on equity (ROE), and debt-to-equity ratio, it is possible to get insights into a company's performance and relative valuation.

By examining the competitive environment, market dynamics, and industry trends, one can ascertain a company's place within its industry and its potential for growth.

Administration and Governance: The management team's experience and track record, corporate governance practices, and strategic initiatives can all be examined to learn more about a company's ability to execute its goals successfully.

Global Economic Issues Broader economic issues like interest rates, inflation, and geopolitical events must be taken into account when evaluating the impact on a company's operations and the general market sentiment.

Chapter 7: Exploring Investment Tools: Stocks, Bonds, Option And More

Equity Securities

As discussed in the introduction, your first step in complying with the five critical functions is to understand different types of securities. This book builds each chapter off the previous one. If you begin studying here, you will build a solid understanding of different securities so you can explain them to your customers.

Understanding how equities work is the foundation to comprehending the more complex material on the test.

Equity Basics

When a corporation needs to raise capital, it issues stocks. Stock is a form of ownership, or equity, in a company in the form of shares. Before covering types of stock, first you must understand the process involved in underwriting, or creating, equities. This section is about how a stock is born, the players involved, and some of the laws you as an applicant must know to pass the Series 7 exam.

There are a lot of fundamental concepts, laws, and functions to memorize within this portion of your preparation for the Series 7 exam. Take your time reviewing this material and use the bold text to study. You will be tested on all the subjects outlined in this section.

Functions

First, this book will discuss some of the people involved in the registration process. As a registered representative you could be working for any of the entities involved in the issuance of securities, so it is important you understand the roles of the players in the underwriting process.

When a stock is issued, the issuing corporation will hire an investment banking firm to manage the issuance of these equities. The investment banking firm will form a syndicate (group) of underwriters to sell the stock with a managing or lead underwriter at the head of this syndicate. A syndicate can hire a selling group if they feel they need help with the selling of securities.

Where the Money Goes

Naturally, all these contributors to a securities sale want a part of the profits to make their efforts worthwhile. A syndicate will make a total profit, or spread, and pays the management fee from this, leaving them with a net profit called the takedown. Looking at the hierarchy chart will help you make sense of how the money trickles down. To understand how this profit is divided up and how to calculate exact profits, look at this example.

Syndicate Agreements

When forming the syndicate, its members will come to a syndicate agreement on who gets paid what and the responsibility each member has to the shares the syndicate commits to. Syndicate agreements are either Eastern Accounts, where responsibility for sales is shared between members, or Western Accounts, where each member is only responsible for their portion of assigned syndicate shares. A typecasts decide the type of agreement based on preference; for Series 7, you simply need to identify how the type of agreement affects individual members' responsibilities.

Example:

George Jones is part of a syndicate group of five underwriters. The group commits to 1,000,000 shares. He has sold his share of 200,000 shares. 100,000 shares remain unsold.

Under an Eastern Account, he would be responsible for selling another 20,000 shares (100,000 divided by five members). Under a Western Account, he would have met his obligation to the syndicate by selling his portion of the total shares, with no commitment to the unsold shares.

Six Steps to Registering Securities

When a corporation decides it wants to issue securities, it must go through six steps to register them.

The six steps in registering securities are:

1. applying to the Securities and Exchange Commission (SEC) that includes the company's name, a summary of its business, a list of its officials, and capitalization.

2. release of the preliminary prospectus, sometimes known as a red herring, to inform prospective investors of the future sale.

3. creating syndicates or underwriting groups.

4. Meetings between the underwriters and the issuing company are held to finalize any agreements. A due diligence meeting is being held here.

5. meeting the standards of "Blue Sky Laws". The company will file a final prospectus and a public offering registration with the state(s).

This is the most basic breakdown of the process involved. To expand on step five, Series 7 expects you to understand Blue Sky Laws and ways to register to comply.

In the 1929 stock market crash, many investors lost their money due to fraudulently represented investments — they were sold worthless investments (or pieces of blue sky, as one judge called them). To protect investors, many states require sellers to register the securities they are selling, providing financial data to aid in buyers' decision making. These registration requirements are known as Blue Sky Laws. For your exam, all you need to know is how a company should register its securities to comply with these laws.

There are three ways a company can register with a state:

1. Coordination: the issuing company files with the SEC and the SEC helps the company file with the state

2. When a security must still file with the state even when it is exempt from the SEC

3. Notification: Established businesses can simply renew their application if they previously registered with the state for a securities offering.

Series 7 will include questions about Blue Sky Laws because these laws focus on investor protection; make sure you understand their purpose and application.

Common Stock

Now that you understand the basic process of underwriting securities, you will move on to different types of equity securities. Common stock is the most basic kind of share in equity and gives its owner a right to vote and dividends if board members decide to distribute them.

Understanding Shares

A corporation may approve the issuance of a number of shares to the public when it conducts its initial public offering (IPO). The entire, maximum number of stock shares that a corporation is permitted to issue is specified in its articles of incorporation as authorized stock.

In order to avoid low initial stock values, businesses typically do not wish to issue all of these shares at once. The issued shares are equities sold in the market as part of an IPO; the business will reserve a portion of the permitted shares.

Companies regularly buy back some of these stocks and keep onto them for a variety of reasons, mostly to manage the stock's value as well as taxes and expenses. Treasury stock refers to the shares that the corporation repurchases. The market's surviving stocks are all excellent stocks. To illustrate how this issue of shares functions, look at diagram 2.2.

How to calculate issued stock:

- Issued stock = treasury stock + outstanding stock

The Series 7 exam will test your ability to calculate each of these types of shares, like in the following example:

Example:

ABC Corporation has issued 1,000,000 stock shares. It has decided to keep 300,000 treasury stock, leaving 700,000 shares in outstanding stocks.

Stockholder Rights

Because holding stock means owning a piece of a company, those stocks hold certain rights, which you are expected to know for your Series 7 exam. This book will cover calculations involved with some of these rights later in this chapter; for now, here are the rights you should know. Please note: these rights apply to common stock only. More information on preferred stock and corresponding rights will be discussed later in this chapter.

These are common stockholder rights:

1. Access to corporate books: a stockholder has the right to see a corporation's balance sheet and income statements.

2. Voting: a common stockholder can vote on stock splits and dividends

3. Share in dividends: a common stockholder has a right to dividends if disbursed.

4. Preemptive rights: right to buy shares before it is offered to others.

5. Residual claims on corporate assets: common stockholders can hold claim to assets in case of the issuing company's liquidation.

Preferred Stock

Preferred stock works much like common stock in the sense it gives the investor ownership in a company. Preferred stock was created because investors often have different risk tolerance, tax needs, and financial objectives. Rights and dividends work differently for preferred stock, which you will learn in this section.

Rights

Preferred stock exists to give stockholders more rights and limit their risk in certain situations, mainly in a volatile market with greater risk of bankruptcy. A company's preferred stock will trade at a different price than common stock, depending on the value the market gives its right at the time.

A preferred stockholder's rights are:

1. Cash dividends regularly (either paid or owed, with exception of straight preferred stock—see "Types of Preferred Stock" for more details)

2. If the underlying company goes bankrupt, preferred stockholders will be paid back their investment before common stockholders

The second preferred stockholder right is most important. Preferred stockholders will be repaid their investment before common stockholders, should the issuing company go bankrupt. You should know that preferred stockholders have no voting rights.

Preferred stockholders' dividends are based on their par value, or face value, at issuance of the stock.

Types of Preferred Stock

To cater to different situations and stockholder preferences, issuers have created several types of preferred stock. These features sometimes benefit the investor, like senior preferred stock for an investor concerned about being repaid in case of bankruptcy. Sometimes the features benefit the issuer, like with callable preferred stock, where the issuer can control its stock price by having the option to buy it back. For your Series 7 exam, you should know the basic characteristics of all of these.

The different types of preferred stock are:

- If the issuer does not pay a dividend, straight preferred stock does not accrue dividends.

- In the case of cumulative preferred stock, if a dividend is not paid, it builds up and becomes due.

- Preferred stock that is convertible at any time into common stock. Conversion ratio is calculated as follows: par value divided by conversion price.

- Callable preferred stock: allows the issuer to repurchase preferred shares whenever they choose.

- Participating preferred stock: dividend paid to investment in common shares.

- In the event of the issuer's insolvency, the investor will be paid out before other preferred stockholders.

- Preferred stock with an adjustable or floating rate: The dividend rate is changed every six months to reflect current interest rates. .

Chapter 8: Debt Securities And Municipal Bonds

How Bonds are Issued into the Market

1. Determine the capital needed: The issuer, which could be a city, business, or government entity, assesses its financial requirements and decides to raise money by selling bonds.

2. Make a plan for the sale of bonds: The issuer determines the key components of the bond offering, including the bond type, maturity date, interest rate, and any special features or conditions. This data is described in the prospectus or bond indenture, a legal instrument.

3. Consult underwriters: The issuer frequently hires an investment bank or a group of underwriters to manage the bond offering. The bond's pricing, structure, and marketing to potential investors are all supported by the underwriters.

4. use caution The underwriters help the issuer execute due diligence to verify that all legal requirements are met, including submitting necessary documents to the right authorities and obtaining necessary licenses.

5. Create the circumstances: The issuer and underwriters come to an agreement on the terms and circumstances of the bond offering, including the face value (or par value) of the bonds, their interest payment schedule, and any covenants or limitations attached to them.

6. Registration of bonds: The Securities and Exchange Commission (SEC) in the US and other pertinent regulatory agencies have the bonds on file. This ensures transparency and compliance with securities laws.

7. Bond advertising The bonds are actively marketed by the underwriters to potential institutional and retail investors. They might host roadshows, distribute promotional materials, and provide investing advice to attract buyers.

8. Bonds' market value The final price at which the bonds will be offered is determined by the underwriters based on investor demand and market conditions. This price may be par (face value), reduced, or higher.

9. The underwriters distribute the bonds to investors in accordance with their orders once the bond price has been decided. The bonds, which are often given to big institutional investors, may be distributed to reduced investors in a smaller amount.

10. Close the deal: The deal is settled between the underwriters and investors by exchanging cash for bonds. This settlement process often occurs a few days after the bond is issued.

11. the list of bonds If the bonds are publicly traded, they may be listed on a stock exchange or an over-the-counter market, and investors may purchase and sell them after the initial issuance.

12. After the bonds are issued, the issuer is responsible for looking after them by restoring the principal amount at maturity and paying periodic interest to bondholders.

Municipal Bonds

Municipal bonds may be issued as securities by state, municipal, and U.S. territory governments. The municipality takes out loans from investors to pay for and maintain infrastructure like roads, sewage systems, hospitals, etc. The interest payments on these bonds are frequently exempt from federal taxation.

Even though you'll probably spend most of your time selling equity assets (stocks), the Series 7 test gives municipal securities a shaky amount of weight.

Taxes serve as bond security for general obligation debts.

Most questions on the Series 7 municipal exam are about general obligation (GO) bonds. You can prepare by carrying out the following.

General GO characteristics

When studying for the Series 7 test, you must know and recall the following specifics of GO bonds:

- They support non-profit facilities financially. Municipalities issue GO bonds to fund or construct projects that don't generate enough money, if any, to assist pay off debt. Schools, libraries, police forces, and fire stations are just a few of the institutions that receive income from GOs.
- They are backed by the municipality's full faith and credit (taxing authority). Municipal liabilities' bonds are backed by local tax receipts.
- They must receive voter approval. Because municipal bonds are backed by local taxes, residents have the opportunity to vote on the proposed project.

Analyzing GO bonds

The Series 7 exam measures your capacity to assess various municipal securities and direct a client toward the optimal option. GO bonds must undergo the same amount of due diligence as other investments. However, because GO bonds are backed by taxes rather than sales of goods and services, there are additional factors to take into account when evaluating the marketability and safety of the offering.

Ascertaining Marketability

The marketability of municipal bonds may be affected by a variety of variables, including the issuer's qualities, factors affecting the issuer's ability to pay, and municipal debt ratios.

Investors should be cautioned to avoid municipal bonds that are difficult to market unless they are ready to assume additional risk. The following other factors could have an impact on bonds' marketability:

- The more secure and marketable a bond is, the better the bond's credit rating.
- Maturity: Shorter maturities improve an issue's marketability.
- Call features reduce the marketability of callable bonds in comparison to non-callable bonds.
- Bonds with higher coupon (interest) rates have a higher marketability when all other conditions are held constant.
- Block size: There is an inverse relationship between block size and the bond's marketability.
- Dollar pricing: A bond's marketability rises with a lower dollar price, all else being equal.
- Bonds are more marketable when the issuer, whether local or national, has a strong track record of prompt bond repayment. Additionally, their debt securities will be more marketable if they have a national reputation for prompt debt repayment rather than just a local one.

- Numerous factors can affect how quickly municipal bonds can be sold on the secondary market, or how liquid they are. Investors would need to think about the issuer's name, the target nation, the bond's rating, the coupon rate, the cost in dollars, the maturity length, etc.
- Support for credit and liquidity: Municipal securities with credit and liquidity support include a letter of credit from a bank that ensures the payment of principle and interest in the event that the municipal issuer is unable to do so. As a result, the issuer is able to sell securities that are secured by credit and liquidity at cheaper rates. This increases security by another level.
- In contrast to corporate bonds, municipal bonds typically have a minimum denomination of $5,000. The minimum denomination of bonds issued by several municipalities is $100,000 or more. Investors will probably have access to municipal bonds with a $5,000 face value more frequently overall.
- Sinking fund: Since there is less chance of default, bonds are more marketable if the issuer has money set aside to redeem them at maturity.
- Insurance: If bonds are guaranteed against default, they are viewed as being extremely secure and are much more marketable. Bond insurance is regarded as enhancing credit.

Municipal bonds' marketability may be impacted by a number of variables. According to the SEC, any substantial changes that can damage the marketability of municipal securities must now be reported to the Municipal Securities Rulemaking Board (MSRB). Significant modifications shall be noted within ten business days after the event.

Debt Management

The municipality's ability to manage debt is one aspect that affects how safe GO bonds are. After taking into account the name of the issuer, you can check the municipality's past issues to verify if it was able to pay its debts on time.

You should take into account the municipality's current debt in addition to its name (and credit history). The net total debt of the municipality includes its direct debt obligations and its commitment to repay a share of other loans.

- Net direct debt is the name for the debt incurred by the municipality. The net direct debt is comprised of both short-term municipal notes and government commitments. Revenue bonds are not accounted for in the overall amount of direct debt because they are self-sustaining.
- Overlapping debt occurs when many authorities in one location have the power to tax the same individuals.

The debt per capita is calculated by dividing the total debt (global, direct, and overlapping) by the population of the municipality (per person). The lower this number, the better it is for an investment.

Collecting taxes, fees, and penalties

Taxes, one of life's few constants, also have an impact on how safe GO bonds are. Investment repayment is funded by sales taxes and property taxes, which are imposed by local governments rather than by the federal government. With the aid of traffic fines and license fees, taxes bring money into municipal coffers and ultimately into the hands of investors.

These are some pertinent elements:

Property values: The primary funding source for GO bonds is ad valorem (property) taxes. Despite the fact that local residents desire low property values, municipal bond holders want property values to be high (at least for tax purposes). As assessed value rises, so do the amount of taxes received and the ease with which the municipality can pay off its debt.

When determining an individual's ad valorem taxes in Series 7 questions, you must always use the assessed value rather than the market value. Ad valorem taxes are calculated using mills, or thousandths of a dollar (one mill is equivalent to $0.001).

Population: It is obviously desirable if there are more taxpayers to support the issuance of bonds. Another very significant factor is the demographic trend. Investors favor increasing population over declining population in a city.

Tax base: The tax base is comprised of the population of the municipality, the assessed value of its properties, and the average annual income of each resident. A bigger tax base is preferable.

Sales per capita: Because sales taxes help finance GO bonds, sales per capita, or the quantity of items the average person purchases, is particularly significant.

Revenue Bonds: Funding Utilities and Other Entities

Revenue bonds are used to finance municipal projects that will generate enough income to pay off the bonds rather than projects that are supported by taxes. These bonds can be used for a variety of things, including student loans, toll highways, airports, hospitals, and utilities.

The construction of a facility for a potential business can be financed by industrial development revenue bonds (IDRs), which can be issued by municipalities. Remember that even when a municipality issues IDRs, they are always backed by the rent payments made by a firm. The corporation guarantees the bonds, hence the bonds' reputation is based on the company's credit rating.

Chapter 9: Life Insurance, Annuities And Retirement Plans

Financial products like life insurance, annuities, and retirement plans are made to offer stability and income during life stages. An overview of each of these goods is provided below:

Life Insurance:

A life insurance policy is an agreement between a person and an insurance provider. The insurance firm receives recurring premium payments from the policyholder in return for providing a death benefit to the policy's beneficiaries in the event of the policyholder's passing. In the event of the policyholder's untimely passing, life insurance is primarily designed to offer financial security and support to their dependents or beneficiaries. There are numerous varieties of life insurance, each with unique characteristics and advantages, such as term life insurance, whole life insurance, and universal life insurance.

Financial agreements known as annuities give a person a consistent income stream over a set time period or for the rest of their life. An individual often makes a one-time investment or ongoing payments into an annuity. Taxes are deferred until the individual decides to begin receiving payments, so the accumulated funds increase tax-deferred. In order to supplement other retirement income sources, such as Social Security or pensions, annuities are frequently utilized as a method for generating income in retirement. There are various annuity varieties, each with their own characteristics and risks, such as fixed annuities, variable annuities, and indexed annuities.

Retirement Plans:
Investment vehicles known as retirement plans assist people in setting aside money for their later years. These programs may be formed by private parties or businesses (like 401(k) plans in the United States) (such as Individual Retirement Accounts or IRAs). Tax benefits are provided by retirement programs to encourage long-term saving. These plans allow for tax-deductible contributions, and investment gain is tax-deferred until withdrawals are made in retirement. The money saved up in retirement accounts is meant to supplement income during retirement and assist people maintain their standard of living after they stop working.

It's crucial to keep in mind that depending on the nation you live in and the laws governing these products, the specifics of life insurance, annuities, and retirement plans may change. To learn about your alternatives and how they can best match your financial requirements and goals, it is advisable to speak with a financial counselor or insurance specialist.

Chapter 10: Financial Risk Management: Diversification, Margin, And More

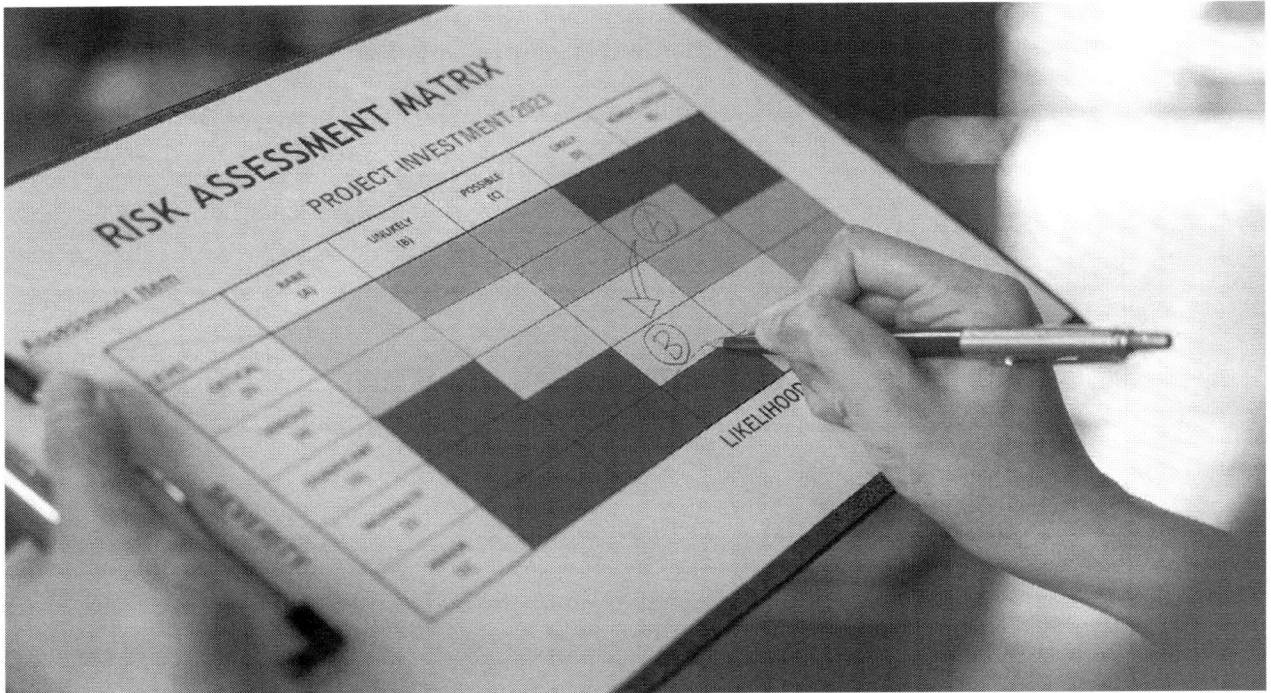

To identify, evaluate, and reduce potential risks in investment and financial activities, financial risk management uses a variety of tools and techniques. Margin and diversity are two crucial components of risk management. Let's examine these ideas and go through some additional crucial components of financial risk management.

Diversification: Spreading investments across many assets or asset classes helps to minimize the effect that the performance of any one investment will have on the portfolio. By diversifying, you can keep a balanced exposure to several sectors, industries, or geographical areas while potentially reducing the risk involved with any one particular investment. The effect of market volatility or unanticipated occurrences that affect a specific asset or industry is lessened through diversification.

Margin: Using borrowed money to purchase securities is known as margin. By using margin, investors can potentially increase returns by leveraging their initial investment. Margin trading does, however, include higher risks. The investor may be asked to contribute more money if the investment's value falls, or they may run the danger of having their position liquidated. Margin trading should be used cautiously because it can amplify gains as well as losses.

Risk evaluation: Prior to making any investment decisions, it's critical to evaluate the investment's risk. This entails assessing variables like market circumstances, business developments, financial results, legal concerns, and other pertinent indications. Making educated decisions and avoiding mistakes requires comprehensive research and analysis.

Risk measurement is essential to effective risk management. Risk is evaluated using a variety of metrics and ratios, such as standard deviation, beta, value at risk (VaR), and conditional value at risk (CVaR). Investors who use these tools are better able to comprehend the potential volatility and downside risks linked to their investment portfolios.

Using financial tools or tactics to mitigate prospective losses in an investment position is known as hedging. Investors can utilize options contracts, for instance, to hedge against unfavorable price changes in the assets in their portfolio. Investors can lessen the impact of unforeseen market occurrences on their investments by hedging.

Asset Allocation: The distribution of investments among various asset classes, such as stocks, bonds, real estate, and commodities, is referred to as asset allocation. A portfolio should be built with consideration for an investor's risk appetite, investment objectives, and time horizon. Effective risk management can be achieved with a portfolio that is properly diversified and has the right asset mix.

Stress testing: To assess how a portfolio or investment strategy might do in challenging circumstances, stress testing entails simulating numerous scenarios, including abrasive market conditions. Stress testing aids in the identification of weaknesses, the evaluation of the investment's resilience, and the improvement of risk management tactics.

Financial risk management is an ongoing activity that requires constant monitoring. It is crucial to regularly analyze investments, market circumstances, and shifts in the risk environment. This enables investors to recognize new risks, change portfolio allocations as necessary, and respond quickly to possible threats.

Keep in mind that financial risk management is a complex subject, so it's best to seek the advice of knowledgeable experts or financial advisors to customize risk management plans to your unique needs and objectives.

Chapter 11: Client Safety And Fraud Prevention

Maintaining trust and integrity in any organization depends on safeguarding customers and preventing fraud. Whether you run a banking institution, an e-commerce platform, or any other kind of business that includes client transactions, it is crucial to put policies in place to safeguard the security of your customers and shield them from fraud. The following are some crucial tactics and procedures for protecting clients and preventing fraud:

Secure Data Protection: Implement robust security measures to protect your clients' personal and financial data. This includes encryption, secure server infrastructure, regular security audits, and compliance with relevant data protection regulations such as the General Data Protection Regulation (GDPR) or the California Consumer Privacy Act (CCPA).

Strong Authentication: Use multi-factor authentication (MFA) for client logins, especially when gaining access to sensitive data or carrying out financial transactions.

By requesting additional information from consumers, such as a one-time password given to their mobile device, MFA offers an extra layer of security.

Informing Clients To assist clients in understanding typical fraud schemes, phishing scams, and best practices for protecting their personal information, provide tools, guidelines, and educational materials. Keep in touch with your clients on a regular basis to alert them of any concerns and safety precautions.
Implement reliable methods for keeping an eye on client transactions and activity. Use machine learning and algorithms to identify suspicious or unusual behavior, such as large or out-of-the-ordinary transactions, and flag them for manual inspection.

Fraud Detection and Prevention: Use fraud detection systems to find possibly fraudulent activity by looking at patterns, behaviors, and transactional data. Implement policies and algorithms that can instantly identify or reject dubious transactions, alerting your fraud prevention staff and your clients for further inquiry.

Regular Auditing and Monitoring: Conduct periodic internal audits to identify vulnerabilities in your systems and processes. Monitor access logs, system logs, and user activities to detect any unauthorized access or suspicious behavior. Promptly investigate and address any anomalies.

Secure Payment Processing: If your business involves financial transactions, work with reputable payment processors and ensure that their systems meet industry security standards. Use secure payment gateways and regularly update your systems to mitigate vulnerabilities.

Strong Password Policies: Encourage clients to use strong, unique passwords and enforce password complexity requirements. Consider implementing password expiration policies and provide guidance on password management best practices.

Phishing Prevention: Educate clients about phishing attacks and how to identify suspicious emails, links, or phone calls. Advise them not to share personal or financial information through unsecured channels and provide a clear process for reporting phishing attempts.

Incident Response Plan: Develop a comprehensive incident response plan that outlines steps to be taken in the event of a security breach or fraud incident. This includes communication protocols, legal obligations, client notification procedures, and remediation measures.

Remember that fraud prevention is an ongoing effort. Stay updated on the latest fraud techniques and security practices, and regularly review and enhance your security measures to adapt to evolving threats.

Chapter 12: Practice Questions

1. Comparatively to statutory voting, cumulative voting is advantageous for:

I. Greater shareholder size

II. Holders of mortgage bonds

III. Smaller shareholders

IV. Bondholders of convertible debt

A.   I only

B.   II and IV

C.   III alone

D.   II and III

2. Which of these benefits of investing in ADRs is NOT one?

A. American dollars are used to pay out the payments.

B. US dollars are used for all transactions.

C. ADRs are governed by anti-fraud laws.

D. There is less currency risk.

3. CMOS is often rated as:

A.   AAA

B.   AA

C.   BBB

D.   SP1

4. Unless otherwise stated, the following are all different forms of state securities registration:

A.   Informative

B.   Collaboration

C.   Qualification

D.   Quantification

5. Keith Coal burner questioned his most recent purchase of municipal bonds in a letter of protest to his broker-dealer. After receiving the complaint, the broker-dealer first:

A.   Repurchase the securities as soon as possible for an amount equivalent to or marginally higher than Keith's buy cost.

B.   Promise to make the client whole

C.   Refund any added markup or commission

D.   Acknowledge the complaint and document any further actions

6. A website that offers nonprofessional investors thorough information on municipal assets, including up-to-the-minute pricing, is known as a municipal securities website.

A.   The Blue Listing

B.   OPRA

C.   EMMA

D.   NASDAQ

7. In which of the following scenarios might an investor sustain an infinite maximum loss?

I.   Short two DIM November 40 puts

II.   400 shares of DIM ordinary stock sold short

III.   Short six DIM November 50 exposed calls

IV.   Short 3 DIM November 50 protected puts

A.   Both I and II

B.   I and III

C.   II and III

D.   II and IV

8. For a speculative investor, a registered representative undertakes the following transactions:

Call 8 on May 30 to purchase 1 GHI.

For $3, sell 1 GHI May 35 call option.

Are these deals suitable for this investor?

A.   It is difficult to know based on the facts provided.

B.   Almost certainly not since the risk is insufficient for a speculative investor.

C.   Option purchases and sales are always acceptable for speculative investors.

D.   It is difficult to generate a profit from these situations.

9. Ben Maverick, who has owned 100 shares of UPP stock for six months, decides to acquire a call on the company with a nine-month maturity. What is Ben's tax situation if the UPP call option expires and he chooses to sell UPP shares four months after the expiry of the call?

A. A capital gain or loss, whether it is short- or long-term.

B. A long-term or short-term capital gain or loss.

C. An investment capital gain or loss on long-term holdings

D. Gains or losses from selling short-term assets, category

10. John Dow and Jane Dough, a couple who are not married, wish to create a bank account in their names as joint tenants with survivorship rights. What comes next should be expected.

A firm executive should be informed right away about the account registration so that FINRA can be contacted.

B. The representative needs to decline to open an account.

C. The agent is required to inform the firm's owner and submit a report to the SEC.

D. The agent may open the account, but only after explaining the terms of the JTWROS account to an unmarried couple.

11. ALL the following must be included in advertisements that contain recommendations EXCEPT:

A.   If the company is a market maker for the proposed security

B.   If the company participated as an underwriter in the security's most recent public offering,

C.   If the company engaged in a recent public offering of securities as a member of the selling group.

D.   If business partners possess options or warrants to purchase the suggested securities

12. If a consumer has a margin account with $18,000 worth of securities, a $7,000 negative balance, and Regulation T is 50%, which of the following statements is FALSE?

A.   The account's purchasing capacity is $4,000.

B.   If the customer withdraws excess equity, the debit balance is reduced by the withdrawal amount.

C.   The account has a surplus balance of $2,000.

D.   The account's holdings have most likely been appreciated.

13. Which sort of margin account demands $25,000 in minimum equity?

A.   A margin portfolio account

B.   A concise account

C.   A trading account for day trading

D.   A business accounts

14. Obtaining a license is necessary before buying or selling options for consumers.:

A.   ODD

B.   OCC

C.   Margin agreement

D.   OPRA

15. The rules of priority, precedence, and parity for bids and offers apply to trading on the.

A.   OTC pink market

B.   Fourth industry

C.   New York Stock Exchange (C)

D.   OTC market

16. Who maintains a fair and orderly market on the New York Stock Exchange trading floor?

A.   Floor brokers

B.   Two-dollar brokers

C.   Designated market makers

D.   Order book clerks

17. Before creating an options account, a consumer must get a disclosure document (n):

A.   Credit contract

B.   OCC

C.   OAA

D.   ODD

18. Date of settlement for municipal bonds:

A.   T+1

B.   T+2

C.   T+3

D.   Up to five business days at the discretion of the buyer

19. Regulation SHO encompasses:

A. Local and U.S. government security margin standards

B. The selling of securities short

C. Margin requirements for commodities

D. Portfolio margining regulations

20. What benefit of including REITs in a customer's portfolio is NOT one of the following?

A. Having a meticulously tended property portfolio.

B. Favorable dividend treatment

C. The possibility of hedging against a decline in the value of other equity securities by using a REIT.

D. Liquidity

21. The formal statement of a municipal bond issue would NOT include the following components.

A. The tagging

B. A summary of the issuer

C. The coupon interest rate

D. A legal opinion

22. Which of the following claims about a variable annuity's annuitization is accurate?

I. The value of each annuity unit has been determined.

II. An annuity's unit count is predetermined.

III. Annuity unit values are erratic.

IV. The annuity units' changeable number.

A.   Both I and II

B.   II and III

C.   II and IV

D.   None of the above

23. Which of the following investments requires a registered representative to provide a written statement of an investor's net worth?

A. Hedge funds, first

B. Fixed annuities

C. Programs with direct participation

D. Municipal bonds that are triple tax-free

24. A customer has shown interest in acquiring stock with a beta of 1.6. You may inform him of that:

A.   The stock is as volatile as the market.

B.   The stock's volatility is lower than the markets.

C.   The stock's volatility exceeds that of the market

D.   Cannot be determined

25. The head and shoulders pattern suggests:

A.   A bearish trend reversal

B.   A change in a negative trend

C.   The stock is traveling horizontally

D.   It might be an excellent moment to sell short.

26. Michael Smith bought one thousand shares of WOW common stock for $26 a share. Six months later, WOW is trading at $60, and Michael anticipates a short-term decrease in the market price. Nevertheless, Michael is certain that WOW is a wonderful firm, and he remains positive about WOW's common shares in general. Which of the following positions would offer Michael protection while still allowing him to create more revenue if his evaluation is accurate?

A.   Sell 1,000 WOW calls short and buy 10 WOW calls maturing in December 1965 for $300 each.

B.   Acquire ten WOW straddles for $60

C.   Sell 10 WOW Dec 65 call options for $300 apiece and set a sell-stop order for 1,000 WOW shares at 57.

D.   Purchase ten WOW Oct 60 puts at $500 apiece

27. One of your clients purchased one OEX Sep 360 put and 100 ARGH shares for $44.10 per share. A few months later, the OEX index is trading at 336, while ARGH is trading at 42.55. What profit will your client make if he sells all his stock and exercises his OEX put?

A. $155

B. $495

C. $1,100

D. $35,395

28. All-or-none orders must be:

A.   Performed promptly in their full or the order is canceled

B.   Completed or the order is canceled

C.   Partly performed promptly or the order is canceled

D.   Partly carried out or the order is canceled

29. For a brokerage business to handle an ACAT, it must be a member of the:

A.   FINRA

B.   NSCC

C.   SIPC

D.   DRS

30. The SMA of a lengthy account is increased by ALL of the following EXCEPT

I.   Transferring assets from the account

II.   Acquiring additional securities for the account.

III.   Receipt of a dividend payment

IV.   A decline in the market value of the account's holdings

A.   I and III

B.   II and IV

C.   I, III, and IV

D.   II, III, and IV

31. At $9 per share, DEF Corporation issued stock to the public. What was the spread if the manager's fee was $0.15 per share, the takedown was $0.50 per share, and the concession was $0.30 per share?

A. $0.45

B. $0.65

C. $0.80

D. $0.95

32. Which of the following are discretionary customer orders?

I.   "Invest 1,000 shares in a fast-growing company"

II.   "Buy or sell 500 LMN shares."

III.   "Buy or sell as many TUV shares as you believe I can manage."

A.   Both I and II

B.   II and III

C.   I and III

D.   I, II, and III

33. Which of the following is true about dark liquidity pools?

I.   They represent institutional and high-end retail clientele.

II.   They reduce the amount of informational transparency regarding securities trading.

III.   Companies that trade in their inventory may be included.

IV.   As exchange transactions, the trades executed by the pools are reported.

A.   Both I and IV

B.   I, II, and IV

C.   I, II, and III

D.   II and III

34. Mutual funds must at the very least distribute financial statements to shareholders.

A.   Each month

B.   Twice monthly

C.   Quarterly

D.   Semiannually

35. What needs to be filled out on a new account application?

I.   Customers' names and addresses

II.   The customer's birth date

III.   The category of account

IV.   The investor's investment goals

A.   Both I and II

B.   I, II, and III

C.   I, II, and IV

D.   I, II, III, and IV

36. What is the minimum amount of assets required for a client to open a prime brokerage account?

A. $100,000

B. $500,000

C. $1,000,000

D. $5,000,000

37. Which of the following advantages of participating in a real estate DPP program is not one?

I. Depreciation

II. Appreciation

III. Depletion

IV. Funds flow

A. Both I and II

B. III and IV

C. I, II, and IV

D. I, II, III, and IV

38. A client owns a substantial amount of Treasury and investment-grade corporate bonds with long maturities. His primary risk concern ought to be:

A. Credit danger

B. Inflationary danger

C. Systemic threat

D. Timing risk

39. If LMN common stock is trading at $44 and has a $2.20 dividend, a current yield of 5%, a PE ratio of 6, and a dividend yield of 5%, then its estimated earnings per share are $4.

A. $0.44

B. $2.73

C. $7.33

D. $8.80

    40. ratio of PE to

A. Earnings per share are split by market price.

B. Dividends per share of common stock paid annually divided by the stock's current market value.

C. Diluted earnings per share divided by annual dividends per share.

D. The sum of preferred dividends less the net revenue divided by the quantity of outstanding common shares.

    41. The following assets are owned by an investor:

50 New York 5% general obligation bonds with a 2030 maturity and an AA rating.

50 6.25 percent revenue bonds for Florida University with a 2031 maturity and an AA grade

50 Nevada Turnpike bonds with a 5.75 percent coupon that mature in 2030 and are rated AA

What kind of diversification does this constitute?

A.   Maturity

B.   Quality

C.   Quantity

D.   Geographical

    42. One DUD Jun 55 put is purchased by a customer at 4.50 when DUD is trading at 53.40. The option is trading at 4.55 bid to 4.65 asking just before expiration.

78

What is the shortfall or surplus if the customer closes his position with a market order?

A. $5 gain

B. $5 loss

C. $160 gain

D. $160 loss

43. A stockholder has shorted XYZ common shares at the age of 55. The investor expects a long-term loss in value as the price of XYZ common shares recently dropped to $30. If an investor wants to protect themselves from a potential price increase, they should:

A.   Buy an XYZ call

B.   Sell an XYZ call

C.   Buy an XYZ put

D.   Buy an XYZ combination

44. Grant Goldbarr purchased 1 ABC 60 put at 3.50 and purchased 100 shares of ABC at 62. Six months later, with ABC trading at 64, Grant closes his put for 0.75 and sells his stock at the market price. What is Grant's gain or loss as a result of these transactions?

A. $75 loss

B. $75 gain

C. $275 loss

D. $275 gain

45. What are the tax repercussions for an investor if they purchase a three-year LEAPS contract at issuance that expires without being exercised?

A. Short-term capital loss

B. Long-term capital gain B.

C. Long-term capital loss

D. Realized capital gains, letter.

46. Without obtaining formal permission, a consumer may give a registered representative permission to act at his discretion.

A. Choosing whether to sell or buy.

B. The expenditure

C. Price and order entry time

D. The number of outstanding shares

47. Which securities from the list below are not exempt?

I. municipal unit investment trust shares

II. The second item is shares of U.S. government bond funds.

III. units of variable annuity accumulation

IV.   A fixed annuity

A.   Both I and II

B.   III alone

C.   III and IV

D.   I, II, and III

48. Which type of fund would be MOST appropriate for Benson Freeman, who has modest resources and wants to get involved in the pharmaceutical industry without focusing just on one or two businesses?

A.   An alternative investment fund

B.   An industry fund

C.   A well-balanced fund

D.   A money-market fund

49. What are the primary tax advantages of a limited partner participating in an oil and gas exploration drilling program?

A.   Tax deductions

B.   Depreciation expenditures

C.   Recourse loans

D.   Intangible expenses of drilling

50. A 60-year-old customer of yours has 60% of their portfolio invested in stocks, 30% in bonds, and 10% in cash equivalents. He must: Using a common approach for allocating strategic assets.

A.   Sell a portion of his bonds and buy more stocks

B.   Sell a portion of his stocks and buy additional bonds.

C.   He should sell his cash equivalents and buy more stocks and bonds.

D.   Cannot be determined from the provided facts.

51. Benson Fringe acquired two LMN 50 calls for three per option. Additionally, Benson acquired 2 LMN 50 puts for $2 per option. At the time of acquisition, LMN was trading at $50.25 a share. LMN was trading at $44.50 just before

expiry, and Benson chose to close his options for their intrinsic value. Without commission, Benson had a:

A. $50 profit

B. $50 loss

C. $100 profit

D. $100 loss

52. Blackrock Securities agrees to underwrite 10 percent of an Eastern account issue for $50 million and sells out its allotment of $10 million. Other firms which took part in the transaction aren't able to sell their bonds due to the weakness of the American market and $25 million of the bonds remain unsold. What is Blackrock Securities' financial obligation?

A. shared responsibility for $25 million

B. $250,000

C. $0

D. $2.5 million

53. Investors of variable life insurance policies who become disabled can be protected via a rider called a(n)

A. early withdrawal rider

B. waiver of premium

C. disability rider

D. none of the above

54. JKLM Corporation has declared a $0.40 dividend, which will be given to stockholders who possess shares as of September 14 on that day. What would happen to Tuesday, September 12's opening pricing for JKLM?

A. It would remain the same.

B. cannot be determined.

C. The dividend amount would be added to it.

D. It would be reduced by the amount of the dividend.

55. Who is responsible for paying the taxes when securities in a Uniform Gifts to Minors Act (UGMA) account are sold for a profit?

A. The little

B. The donor

C. The keeper

D. The guardian or parent

56. a person who wants to put money into a somewhat secure DPP. Which of these would you suggest to him investing in the least?

A real estate partnership that invests in undeveloped land

B. a program for developing oil and gas

C. a program for generating money from oil and gas.

D. a program for leasing equipment

57. All these activities are a registrar's function EXCEPT

A. ensuring that the outstanding shares do not exceed the number of shares on the corporation's books

B. auditing the transfer agent

C. accounting for the number of shares outstanding

D. transferring shares into the name of the new owner

58. These details must be included in the preliminary prospectus. EXCEPT

A. the purchase price.

B. the objective of the issuer's fund-raising

C. a warning that information in the preliminary prospectus may change before the official prospectus is published.

D. The background and financial standing of the issuer

59. Which of these circumstances necessitates the filing of a currency transaction report by a broker-dealer?

A. A consumer wires $25,000 from his own account to start an account.

B. A consumer deposits $14,000 in cash to start an account.

C. A client used a cheque from a joint account to pay $20,000 for stock.

D. A client deposits bonds for a company having a par value of $30,000.

60. An investment is said to be counter-cyclical if it travels against the direction of the economic cycle. Investments with a history of being counter-cyclical are included.

A. gold stock'

B. shares of a food company

C. Utility stock

D. medicinal stock

61. On a competitive bid for a new municipal underwriting, the difference between the syndicate bid and the reoffering price is the

A. bid price

B. offering price

C. spread

D. discount price

62. In the first margin deal, a shareholder purchases 100 shares of WXY at a price of $24 apiece. What is the transaction's margin call?

A. $1,800

B. $2,400

C. $2,000

D. $1,200

63. DIM, Inc. is providing 800,000 shares of stock owned by selling stockholders in addition to 1 million shares of new stock. This is an offering (n)

A. combined offering

B. primary offering

C. IPO

D. secondary offering

64. Without the assistance of a broker-dealer, a securities transaction between ABC Bank and DEF Insurance Company would be a

A. first market trade

B. second market trade

C. third market trade

D. fourth market trade

65. The second market is

A. Institutional trading without employing a broker-services. dealer's

B. listed financial instruments traded on an exchange.

C. OTC trading of listed securities.

D. OTC trading of unlisted securities

66. A dealer purchases 1,000 shares of HIJK for its own stock at $17.50 per share. A few weeks later, the dealer offers one of his customers 1,000 shares of HIJK at the quoted price of $16.80 to $17.00. Which of the following prices forms the basis for the dealer's markup?

A. $17.50

B. $17.25

C. $17.00

D. $16.80

67. A broker-dealer is acting as a broker when he makes a market in a certain security (n)

A. agent

B. broker

C. principal

D. syndicate member

68. Trader enters a quote between $17.10 and $17.25. A consumer asks the market maker to sell them 1,000 shares of stock. What portion of the shares must the market maker sell?

A. 100

B. 500

C. 200

D. 1000

69. All of these, except for one, are probably a part of an equipment leasing partnership.

A. moving trucks.

B. constructive equipment

C. computers

D. oil well drill heads

70. Ben Philp spends 80 for a fresh OID municipal zero-coupon. What will happen to Ben's taxes if he holds the bond until it matures?

A. $200 capital gain

B. $0

C. $200 ordinary income over the time the bond is held to maturity

D. Non of the above

71. On January 20, 2019, Mary Whitehead bought a convertible bond from LTSBR Corporation for 95. On January 21, 2022, she changes her bond into stock at a conversion price of $40. For tax purposes, if the common stock is trading at $42 and the bond is trading at 104, the transaction will result in

A. a $10 gain

B. a $10 loss

C. a $90 gain

D. neither a gain nor a loss

72. Currently, the price of XYZ trades between 24.10 and 24.25. In XYZ, at which of the following prices might a designated market maker make a bid?

A. 24.25

B 24.12

C. 24.1

D. 24.27

73. The first payment is an early payment if the first coupon payment is due on December 1st but the official statement is dated May 1.

A. normal payment for a seven-month bond

B. mistake printed on the official statement.

C. short coupon

D. long coupon

Chapter 13: Correct Answers

1. **C** - By pooling their ballots, shareholders can cast their votes for anybody they like through cumulative voting. For the purposes of illustration, suppose a shareholder had 1,000 common shares and there were four candidates for director. The shareholders might cast all 4,000 votes (1,000 shares, 4 candidates) for a single candidate if they so chose. Cumulative voting could enable smaller shareholders to participate in the board of directors.

2. **D** - ADRs, or American Depositary Receipts, are designed to make it simpler to trade foreign assets on American markets. ADRs are subject to currency risk since dividends must be translated from foreign currencies to dollars on the distribution date. Currency changes have a substantial impact on the ADR's trading price and can reduce the value of dividends and/or the shares.

3. **A** - CMOs are often rated AAA since they are backed by house mortgages, which are regarded to be quite safe (although not as safe as in past years).

4. **D** - Unless exempt, securities must be registered at both the state and federal levels. There are three sorts of state registration: notice, coordination, and qualification.

5. **D** - After receiving Keith's written complaint, the municipal securities broker-dealer must acknowledge receipt of the complaint and document any actions taken to remedy it. Every broker-dealer shall maintain a complaint file for each client and maintain accurate records of all interactions and activities related to a complaint.

6. **C** - EMMA (Electronic Municipal Market Access) is a consolidated online resource that retail investors can use to get important information about municipal assets. This website provides official statements for the majority of new municipal bond issues and real-time access to the pricing of existing municipal bonds.

7. **C** - It's important to understand that option sellers, sometimes referred to as short sellers or writers, run a higher risk than buyers, whose risk is capped at the amount of their investment. Sellers of put options do not, however, have basically infinite maximum loss potential because put options only enter the money when the stock price drops below the striking price, which can only be $0, and this can only occur when the stock price declines. The highest loss potential for sellers of uncovered calls is limitless because call options become in the money when the stock price rises over the strike price, compelling the seller to purchase the shares at an ever-rising price. Additionally, investors who short the stock as described in Statement II face an unbounded maximum loss potential because they have taken a negative position and will lose money when the security's price increases and nothing is preventing this from happening. Because they have the stock to deliver in the event the option is exercised, investors who sell covered calls do not expose themselves to an illimitable maximum loss.

8. **D** - These transactions are inappropriate for any investment since the investor can't benefit. Because the investor purchased the May 30 call option for $8, you must plot $800 on the **"Money Out"** side of the chart (8 premium 100 shares per option). Next, place $300 (3 premium 100 shares each option) on the "Money In" side of the chart since the option was sold for $300. Since the investor has $800 out and $300 in, their maximum loss potential is $500 ($800 - $300). To get the best benefit, you must use both choices. Due to "calls identical," the exercised strike prices must be placed below their corresponding premiums in the chart. Place $3,000 (30 striking prices 100 shares every option) and $3,500 (35 strike prices 100 shares per option) beneath its premium of $800 and $300, respectively. Since the "Money In" and "Money Out" sides of the chart each equal $3,800, it is necessary to add up the sides to determine that the investor cannot earn a profit.

9. **C**. - Remember that short-term profits or losses are those that occur in less than one year. Ben's holding period for the share that he acquired is unaffected by his

acquisition of a call option. Because Ben has held the shares for 19 months (1 year and 7 months), the sale would result in a long-term capital gain or loss.

10.   **D** - There are no laws that prevent two single people from opening a JTWROS account. However, the registered representative must take all necessary measures to guarantee that the unmarried individuals are informed of the consequences in the event that one account holder passes away. For instance, in a JTWROS-registered account, Jane Dough, the other tenant, rather than the deceased party's estate, gets the deceased party's ownership stake in the account if John Dow, one of the engaged parties, dies.

11.   **D** - Advertisements that incorporate the company's suggestions are not required to state whether the firm worked as a selling group since members of selling groups have no financial risk.

12.   **B** - This margin account is long because it has a debit balance; short accounts have a credit balance. Setting up a lengthy margin account formula is the simplest solution to address these types of margin issues. Since the LMV is $18,000 and the DR is $7,000, the EQ must be $11,000. Then, you must compare what the investor should have in equity to be at 50 percent (Regulation T) of the LMV to what the investor has in equity. Standard Regulation T requires a 50% EQ; thus the investor must have $9,000 in EQ to meet this requirement. Nevertheless, given that the investor has $11,000 in equity, the surplus equity is $2,000.

13. **C** - The initial margin required for a day trading account is $25,000, and to continue trading, the investor must maintain a minimum account balance of $25,000. A relatively new type of margin account bases the required margin on the overall risk of the portfolio. The portfolio margin is only accessible to a select group of participants since it necessitates a particular level of expertise and a minimum equity of roughly $150,000.

14.   **A** - Due to the higher risks involved with investing in options, such as the potential for losing the entire investment or experiencing an unlimited maximum loss, all investors are required to obtain an ODD (Options Risk Disclosure Document) before to making their first transaction. The ODD does not serve as promotional material; it explains the risks associated with option investing. The ROP (Registered Options Principal) must authorize the account after the customer receives the ODD. The customer must finish the transaction and deliver an OAA in addition to signing it (Options Account Agreement).

15.   **C** - The NYSE floor auction rules of priority (highest bid and lowest ask first), precedence (if orders are at the same price, the order that came in first is executed first), and parity (if all other factors are equal, the larger order is executed first) allow for the efficient execution of orders when multiple bids or offers are made at the same price at the same time.

16.   **C** - On the NYSE trading floor, the Designated Market Maker (DMM or Specialist) is responsible for ensuring a fair and orderly market.

17.   **D** - A consumer must obtain an ODD before opening an options account and starting to trade options (Options Disclosure Document or Options Risk Disclosure Document). The characteristics and risks of options trading are discussed in this essay.

18.   **B** - Equities, corporate bonds, and municipal bonds all settle on T+2 days (2 business days after the trade date). On the settlement date, the issuer updates its records, and certificates are given to the buyer's brokerage house.

19.   **B** - Regulation SHO covers short sale laws. According to SHO guidelines, all order tickets must be characterized as short sales rather than long sales, which occur when an investor sells assets they already own. Additionally, all brokerage firms are required to create standards for locating, obtaining, and delivering short-sold assets.

Before completing a short sale, all brokerage companies must verify that the security can be located and delivered by the delivery date.

20.   **B** - Like the majority of other investment industry products, the portfolios of REITs are skillfully managed. Due to the frequently negative link between the real estate market and stock prices, many investors employ REITs as potential hedges against a market slump. REITs usually have a high level of liquidity, too. However, REITs do not benefit from dividend tax advantages.

21.   **A** - The prospectus for a business issue is similar to the official statement for a municipal bond sale. An official statement contains the terms of the offering, the underwriting spread, information on the bonds and the issuer, the offering price, the coupon rate, a feasibility statement, and the legal opinion.

22. **B** - When an investor takes money out of a variable annuity, the accumulation units are converted into a specific amount of annuity units. The value of the annuity units is affected by the performance of the assets maintained in the separate account, though.

23.   **C** - Since direct participation programs (limited partnerships) may ask limited partners to provide additional funds above and beyond their initial commitment, investors are needed to present proven proof of their net worth. The investor has agreed to become a limited partner by signing the subscription agreement with the general partner.

24.   **C** - The beta of a stock indicates how volatile it is compared to the market. You may anticipate your stock's price to rise by the same percentage if the market rose by 5% over a given time period because it has a beta of 1. You anticipate that the price of your stock will decrease by 5% if the market drops by the same percentage. If a stock's beta value is higher than 1, it is more volatile than the market. Your

present stock has a beta of 1.6, which suggests that if the market climbed or decreased by 10% over a given period, you should anticipate a price change of 16% in your stock. A stock that is less volatile than the market would have a beta value below 1.

25.   **B** - An inverted head and shoulders pattern, sometimes referred to as a head and shoulders bottom pattern, is a positive indication that the stock has reached its low point and is beginning to move in the other direction. In other words, a head and shoulders bottom pattern signals a trend change and is bullish.

26.   **C** - Selling covered options on his current 1,000 WOW shares could bring Michael a profit. Additionally, by putting a sell-stop order close below the market price, Michael is protected from suffering a huge loss in the event that WOW's price drops drastically.

27.   **B** - Your client bought 100 shares of ARGH at 44.10, thus you must enter $4,410 (100 shares at 44.10) in the graph's "Money Out" area. Then, for $4.50, your client purchased an OEX put. You must thus enter $450 (4.50 shares for every 100 options) in the "Money Out" column. You must enter $4,255 (100 shares at 42.55 stock price) in the "Money In" column of the chart if your client closes a stock position at that price (to close indicates to do the reverse; if he initially purchased, to close he must sell). You must add the $1,100 profit in the "Money In" column since the option you are working with settles in cash rather than delivery of the underlying asset. Considering that put options are for 100 shares and are in the money when the stock price declines by 11 points (360 - 349) from the strike price, the $1,100 can be obtained. You discover that your client has made $495 profit when you sum the two sides.

28.   **B** - Contrary to fill-or-kill (FOK) and immediate-or-cancel (IOC) instructions, all-or-nothing (AON) commands are not required to be carried out immediately.

However, they must be fully fulfilled, or the order will be canceled, just as FOK orders. Until they are implemented or cancelled, AON orders are regarded as active.

29.   **B** - For a brokerage business to perform an ACAT (Automated Customer Account Transfer), it must be a member of the NSCC (National Securities Clearing Corporation). When a brokerage business is a clearing firm, the firm assumes financial responsibility if a client fails to pay for a deal or fails to deliver sold certificates.

30.   **B** - The wording of this question makes it difficult to answer. Before answering the question, we recommend writing **"increases SMA," "decreases SMA,"** or **"does not affect SMA"** next to each alternative response.

● The sale of securities in a margin account raises the SMA by half the amount of the transaction and reduces the debit balance by the same amount (increases SMA).

● The acquisition of new securities in a long margin account does not influence the SMA until the purchasing power is used, which cannot be assumed (does not modify SMA).

● Deposits of cash dividends or cash payments into the margin account raise the SMA by the amount of the deposit (increases SMA).

● The SMA is unaffected by a fall in the market value of the securities. Remember, you don't lose SMA until you utilize it (doesn't modify SMA).

Now that you understand this section, reread the question to see what it is asking. Statements II and IV are the only ones that do not raise the SMA since this is an EXCEPT question.

31. **B** - The spread is equal to the sum of the manager's fee ($0.15) and the takedown ($0.50), or $0.65. The selling concession is deducted from the takedown and not factored into the spread formula.

32.   **D** - All of the mentioned Roman numeral options would be considered discretionary orders and would need the buyer to execute a formal Power of Attorney for acceptance. To avoid the requirement for a Power of Attorney, the client must supply or agree to the number of shares (or bonds), the purchase or sale direction, and the exact security. Execution of discretionary orders does not need vocal agreement from the consumer.

33.   **C** - Dark liquidity pools perform trades as over-the-counter (OTC) transactions, not exchange transactions. Dark liquidity pools are pools of institutions, huge retail customers, and companies selling their inventory. Due to the anonymity of customers and account sizes, dark pools undermine market transparency.

34.   **D** - Mutual funds are required by the Investment Company Act of 1940 to provide shareholders with semiannual reports. Think "AIM" to keep in mind how frequently account statements should be sent:

A = Account Active (monthly)

I represent a "inactive account" (quarterly)

Mutual fund, or M (semiannually)

35.   **D** - All the specified information must be included on the new account form. In addition, you need the Social Security number (or tax ID of a firm), the profession and kind of business, bank references, net worth, yearly revenue, and the signatures of the registered representative and a principal.

36.   **B** - Your customer must have at least $500,000 in investable assets to open a premium brokerage account. However, if the account is opened via a financial advisor, the minimum deposit is a mere $100,000. Prime brokerage businesses condense information from all of the customer's brokerage accounts into a single statement.

37.   **C** - Investors can receive cash flow, the chance for appreciation, and depreciation deductions from real estate DPPs (direct participation programs - limited partnerships), but not depletion. Depletion only affects partnerships that deal in inherently exhaustible commodities, such as oil and gas.

38.   **B** - All long-term bonds are susceptible to inflation (purchasing power risk). Inflationary risk is the possibility that the return on investment will fall short of inflation. Investors should make equity investments to decrease the risk of inflation. Over the long term, stocks have performed significantly better than inflation.

39.   **C** - To calculate the earnings per share (EPS) of a company, divide the firm's price by its PE (price-earnings) ratio.

40.   **A** - Technical analysts can use the PE ratio to identify whether a company is overpriced or underpriced. To establish whether an investment opportunity is present, they frequently analyze the PE ratios of other businesses operating in the same sector. In actuality, the lower the PE value, the better. A company's earnings per share (EPS) is more likely to be high in relation to its share price when its PE ratio is low.

41.   **D** - Given that the investor bought 50 of each bond, that they were all rated AA, and that they all mature around the same time, you can rule out age, quality, and number as plausible options. The investor's funds serve as an example of regional diversity because the bonds are issued by a range of U.S.-based issuers.

42.   **A** - Even while you might not need an alternatives chart to figure out the answer to this question, creating one is a great skill to master and will, in our opinion, lower your error rate. First, you must enter $450 (4.50 100 shares per option) in the "Money Out" portion of the chart because the buyer paid $4.50 for the option. Next, since you bought the option at the asking price and sold it at the bid price, you must close the option at $4.55. The customer must reverse his earlier actions in order to shut the option; if he bought the option, as in this case, he now needs to sell it. As

97

a result, $455 must be included in the graph's "Money In" column. As he made $455 by selling the option and spent $450 to buy it, it is now obvious that the customer made $5.

43.   **A** - To hedge is to protect. The investor should buy XYZ call options if he wishes to hedging his position. Remember that the investor is short XYZ and will eventually need to buy the stock to cover his short position. An investor who purchases a call option on XYZ has the option to repurchase XYZ at a predetermined price, protecting the position and preventing an unlimited maximum loss possibility.

44.   **A** – Since Grant purchased the put for $350 (3.50 100 shares per option) and the stock for $6,200 (62 100 shares), you must enter "350" and "6,200" in the "Money Out" column. Next, Grant sold the stock for $6,400 (64 100 shares) and closed the option for $75 (0.75 100 shares per option) by selling the stock he had initially purchased. Therefore, you must enter "$6,400" and "$75" in the "Money In" column of the chart. The sum of the two sides reveals that he lost $75.

45.   **C** - Options are always subject to taxation as capital gains or losses. This investor lost money because he acquired an option that expired worthless. Because the investor held LEAP for more than a year, the loss is considered a long-term capital loss.

46.   **C** - Without discretionary authority, registered representatives are unable to choose which securities to purchase or sell, how many shares or dollars to acquire, or whether a client should buy or sell. However, without a duly executed power of attorney, registered representatives may fix the cost or timeframe of an order.

47.   **D** - It is necessary to distinguish between exempt and nonexempt securities. In other words, nonexempt securities must be registered with the SEC. Variable annuities, which involve investment risk, are non-exempt securities under the Securities Act of 1933 and must be registered before being sold to the general public. In a similar vein, unit trusts and mutual funds do not qualify for exemption,

even though the underlying municipal and U.S. government assets do. However, a fixed annuity is an insurance product that is not required to be registered with the SEC. Due to the assured payoff, this is not viewed as a security.

48.   **B** – You would do best with a specialty or sector fund that invests at least 25 percent of its assets in a certain area or industry.

49.   **D** - Investors in an oil and gas exploratory (wildcatting) program get a tax deduction for intangible drilling costs (IDCs), which are the expenditures incurred in obtaining the oil. IDCs include stuff like labor and surveys. IDCs are costs that are deductible in the year they occur.

50.   **B** - As investors mature, they should begin rebalancing their portfolios away from equities and towards bonds and cash equivalents such as money-market securities. It is believed that senior investors cannot afford to assume as much risk. The traditional asset allocation methodology advises subtracting the individual's age from 100 to estimate the proportion of his portfolio that should be invested in equities. Given the investor's age of 60, he should have 40 percent (100–60) of his portfolio invested in equities and the remainder in bonds and cash equivalents.

51. D

52. B

53. D

54. A

55. A

56. D

57. A

58. B

59. A

60. C

61. C

62. A

63. D

64. D

65. C

66. C

67. A

68. D

69. B

70. D

71. B

72. D.

Conclusion

I want to underline the important message that has been weaved throughout "Series 7 Exam Prep" in order to ensure that it will have a lasting impression. Together, we've set out on a journey to arm you with the knowledge and abilities you'll need to ace the Series 7 exam and forge a successful career in finance.

In this thorough guide, we have covered a wide range of crucial subjects that are necessary for passing the Series 7 exam. To ensure a thorough understanding of the properties and pricing of securities, we dug deep into their basics, covering everything from stocks and bonds to options and futures. We clarified the essential laws and guidelines that control the securities business by demystifying the complicated world of regulatory organizations and compliance. To provide you a thorough picture of the options available to investors, we also examined the ins and outs of investment vehicles like mutual funds, annuities, and alternative investments.

Not only have we discussed the fundamentals, but we have also delved into more complex subjects that call for a deeper comprehension. We looked at options techniques, margin trading, and portfolio analysis to provide you the knowledge you need to make wise choices and develop customized investment plans for your clients. We also spent a lot of time discussing the professional obligations and ethical issues that come with being a financial professional, giving you the knowledge and tools you need to uphold the highest standards of integrity in your work.

We have given you a thorough and in-depth road map to success in order to fulfill our pledge to help you through the Series 7 exam preparation process. We have demystified difficult ideas, simplified complex subjects into knowledge that is palatable, and presented examples from the real world to show how they may be applied. We have attempted to strengthen your understanding and increase your confidence in handling the exam by repeatedly emphasizing crucial concepts.

Above all, I want you to learn from this book that hard work and dedication are the cornerstones of success. You can pass the Series 7 test with flying colors by devoting the necessary time and effort to studying the material presented in this manual, fully understanding the concepts, and diligently putting your knowledge into practice with sample questions and mock exams. Have confidence in your skills and knowledge, and go into the exam with a cool, collected head.

Remember that this book is only a steppingstone as you start your career in the financial sector. Your continuing growth and development will be fueled by your appetite for education, your dedication to excellence, and your commitment to provide your clients with honesty. It has laid the groundwork for your future success.

It is now time for you to go on, face the Series 7 exam with confidence, and seize the exciting prospects that lie ahead in your career, equipped with the knowledge you have gained from this book. I hope that this book has been a helpful resource on your path to becoming an informed and well-respected financial expert. I wish you the best of luck in all of your pursuits.

BONUS 1: Tips To Start Your Career

Congratulations on passing the Series 7 exam! It's a significant achievement and an important step towards launching your career in the financial industry. Here are some tips to help you get started:

1. Research and Understand Job Opportunities:

Take the time to research different career paths and job opportunities available to individuals who have passed the Series 7 exam. This will help you identify the areas you're most interested in and guide your job search.

2. Network: Networking is crucial in any industry, especially in finance.

Reach out to professionals in the field, attend industry events, and join relevant professional organizations. Building relationships and connections can open doors to job opportunities and provide valuable guidance and mentorship.

3. Update Your Resume and LinkedIn Profile:

Tailor your resume to highlight your Series 7 qualification and any relevant experience or skills you possess. Ensure your LinkedIn profile is up to date, professional, and showcases your expertise and qualifications.

4. Apply for Jobs:

Start applying for entry-level positions that align with your career goals. Look for positions at brokerage firms, investment banks, asset management companies, or financial advisory firms. Leverage job boards, industry-specific websites, and your network to find suitable opportunities.

5. Prepare for Interviews:

Review common interview questions and practice your responses. Be prepared to discuss your Series 7 exam experience, your knowledge of financial products and regulations, and how you would apply that knowledge in a practical setting. Showcase your communication skills and demonstrate your ability to work in a team.

6. Continuously Learn and Stay Informed:

The financial industry is constantly evolving, so it's important to stay updated on industry trends, regulations, and new products. Subscribe to financial publications, follow industry influencers on social media, and consider pursuing additional certifications or designations to enhance your skills and knowledge.

7. Develop Strong Work Ethics:

Building a successful career requires dedication, commitment, and a strong work ethic. Be proactive, take initiative, and go the extra mile to deliver quality work. Demonstrate your willingness to learn, collaborate with colleagues, and take on new challenges.

8. Seek Mentorship:

Find a mentor within the industry who can provide guidance, support, and valuable insights. A mentor can help you navigate your career, provide advice, and help you develop your skills and knowledge further.

9. Embrace Continuous Professional Development:

Never stop learning and improving your skills. Seek opportunities for professional development, attend workshops, webinars, and industry conferences. Consider pursuing advanced certifications like the CFA (Chartered Financial Analyst) or CFP (Certified Financial Planner) to enhance your career prospects.

10. Be Patient and Persistent:

Starting a career in finance may take time and patience. Be persistent in your job search, and don't be discouraged by rejection. Stay motivated, keep refining your skills, and seize any opportunity that comes your way.

Remember, building a successful career is a journey that requires hard work, dedication, and continuous learning. Stay focused, embrace opportunities for growth, and keep striving for excellence. Best of luck in your career endeavors!

BONUS 2: Online Resources To Help You Pass The Exam

How to Pass the Series 7 Exam by Knowing the Series 7 Exam. Exam introduction by the Series 7 Guru

LIVE Q&A Series 7 exam and ALL FINRA/NASAA Exams

Series 7 Exam Free Project: Investor Profile 2022

Series 7 Exam Prep: Test Taking Tips, Tricks & Memory Aids courtesy of the Series 7 Guru

BONUS 3: #6 Practice Test Simulation Series 7

Manufactured by Amazon.ca
Bolton, ON